LEADERSHIP BASICS

Tools for Leadership Success

By Audra Taylor

I0500316

Leave Your Review of The Book At:

amazon.com/author/curtailer

Claim your free gift:

http://www.taylorsuccessjournal.com/free

Learn more at: www.taylorleadershipbasics.com

Leadership Basics by Audra Taylor

INTRODUCTION

I was in college when I first pondered the concept of leadership, and questioned if leaders were born or made.

When I was being interviewed by the leadership honor society, Omicron Delta Kappa, one of their questions was "Do you believe leaders are born or made?" And that question has stuck with me throughout my career.

I am some who has naturally assumed leadership roles, even in casual situations. I was certain I was "born this way". But, is it that simple? Is it confidence, arrogance, kindness, nurturing, or something else?

I've conducted many social experiments along the way. Standing back and deliberately forcing others to step into leadership roles (this is not inherently easy to do for me). I'd say there are easily 20 percent of the population that could stand up and naturally be leaders, but they are shadowed by some people who "steal" the spotlight.

In this book, I am looking to dig into this concept of leadership. What are leadership styles? What do people mean when they say, "what is your leadership style?"

Another common question that comes up in business is what is the difference between leadership and management. Can you be a good manager, but not a good leader, and vice-versa?

I've tried to pepper the book with facts and historical examples, as well as some anecdotes from my own experience. In my 25 years of leadership and management experience, I have seen great leadership, poor leadership, and absence of leadership.

My hope is by sharing these experiences, we can continue to grow learn and build a new generation of strong, innovative leaders.

CHAPTER 1: WHAT IS LEADERSHIP

As Napoleon Bonaparte had once said, 'a leader is a dealer of hopes'. A good leader has the ability to choose the best people to accomplish difficult tasks and he also has the patience to guide his subordinates. A leader is a great visionary, and great analytical skills.

Leadership is a process and not just a designation. A leader gathers and guides people to support his ideas and policies to obtain better results. It can be difficult at times to get your work done without a strong support network.

Since ages past, leaders are getting things accomplished by making use of apt and organized work forces. If you have keen interest in leadership and its aspects, you have to understand that a leader can motivate the right type of people to give their best for accomplishing a common goal.

Yes, it is true that leaders may not succeed all the time, but motivating people to achieve a common goal is the heart and soul of leadership. People may disagree with their leader's opinions, or may not want to pay heed to his ideas, but this challenge is the driving force behind establishing a successful leadership strategy.

Leadership has its own share of responsibilities. Successful delegation and management is key to large scale success.

While being in charge can be stressful, you can learn to make leadership fun. I've found that managing and mentoring staff is what truly brings joy to my life.

This of leadership not just as a gift but also as an art that needs to be cultivated. Many people think that leaders are born, but be assured that leadership qualities can also be cultivated. It is all about learning some key skills and implementing them as and when opportunity calls.

It is all about how well you use your intelligence and how much patience you can develop. You may not be able to attain all the required skills, but you can devise your own methodology as you gain experience. I've seen more leaders make critical errors when jumping to conclusions, or jumping in too soon to "save" a situation.

One word of caution to an aspiring leader is to remember that 'boss' is not an alternate word for a leader. Successful leaders very often have to put the needs or others or the organization over their own needs. This is not an easy thing, to go against our human instinct of self-preservation, and put the needs of others ahead of ours.

A "boss" is a person who pushes people around to get the work done, but a leader is the person who motivates people to want to get the same work done, and done well. Can you see the difference?

Does the word "job" connote business or corporate responsibilities alone? No. A job could be party planning, quarterbacking a football game, or conducting lectures or seminars. The requirements of leadership vary immensely according to the different jobs that have to be accomplished.

Leadership deals with two fundamental aspects, what are the tasks that need to be performed and the group of people who are to be used for the accomplishment of the same task. If you are alone on a job scene then you cannot be a leader as you will have no group that will follow you.

Similarly, if you have a group but there is no specific job to be accomplished then in this situation, no one can be a leader.

A leader is responsible for mostly two things, one is to get the task accomplished and the other thing which needs careful attention is to hold the team together. This is a lot easier said than done.

I love this quote by Robert Half. He said, "Delegating work works, provided the one who is delegating works, too!"

Leadership, Then and Now

If you asked me if leadership has changed over the years? I would say, "Yes, it certainly has." The conventional strategies and approaches we once used to lead a group have changed significantly over time.

We used to believe that a leader in any organization or field should lead and manage at the same time. But of late this conventional view has seen some transformation and management is no longer directly proportional to leadership.

Back in the day, our leaders were in the position to execute complete authority but nowadays, leaders are no longer regarded as authority figures, but as agencies who can promote new ideas and directions in any organization. This new concept of leadership helps in a great way to develop proper communication channels so that new avenues can be opened to accomplish certain things.

Strategic choices were always made by leaders but today anyone from a group can promote ideas. Previously the leaders were less participative in group activities, but today leaders are involved in several key processes of certain events.

A leader should be able to approach even those people who are not supposed to report to him directly. Leaders once strived only to motivate others and their sole purpose was to ensure profit. You should remember that leadership has nothing to do with management of people.

Today the meaning of leadership has changed. Conventionally, the idea of leadership was often confused with the concept of power. The leader was often regarded as a person who could dominate a large mass of people through persuasion or brute force.

In today's world, which is mainly knowledge driven, the word 'power' has got a new meaning altogether. If you have innovative ideas and promotional skills to assess different projects, this serves as the best basis for leadership.

If a person has specialized knowledge about certain business fields, he can certainly alter the business scenario. In such cases, he will be accepted as a natural leader. This kind of leadership is known as 'thought leadership'.

Previously leadership was almost regarded to be perpetual, once a leader always a leader. Now leadership is thought as an occasional act. This is no more a position or role to be carried to the bitter end. This paradigm shift has helped to inculcate creativity in leadership and has banished the monotonic nature of conventional leadership.

The new age leadership is based on the challenges to the status quo. The pragmatic youth are encouraged to find a better solution to the problems at hand.

Unlike business leadership, the modern day thought leadership or bottom-up leadership is inspired by the actions of people like Martin Luther King Jr. The demonstrations staged by him, had tremendous impact on the decisions of US government.

The conventional ideas of leadership have focused on power rather than on ideas and creativity. Being a leader is not about being a boss but it about being a facilitator to achieve goals.

Today leadership involves taking a firm stand for the ideals you believe in. Your aim as a leader should be to make people think and act differently than what they are accustomed to. Only this can make a difference in their lives. It is about kindling a fire that symbolizes the thought, 'together we can and we will make it.'

The new age mantra for a successful leadership is best quoted by Harold Geneen, "Leadership is an attitude that is practiced through actions and not so by words".

A leader should have faith in his/her subordinates and should always respect them. He should make them feel important. A good leader has to have clear vision of the day ahead and at the end of the day he should have had gained insight by retrospective, which is important while taking decisions on future plans.

Good communication is necessary for every leader. He should be able to fathom roles of a coach, a teacher, and a supporter.

He should prepare for every situation, because decisions taken on the fly can prove to be disastrous in the long run. He should also give proper attention to the suggestions given by others and try to focus on the merits of these ideas.

No one likes to be criticized in public, a good leader always criticizes the ideas, and not the person, and that too in private. He should strike a balance between profession and ethics, and treat all people alike. To maintain a playful and light atmosphere within group a leader needs to have a good sense of humor.

If you have a plan along with an enthusiastic team to carry it out, this may not necessarily end in successful completion of job. Without proper priorities or guidelines for actions in any plan, things tend to go awry. A successful leader prioritizes actions very carefully.

A leader is always on guard for his shortcomings and works rigorously and patiently on self-development. Leadership is no longer a phenomenon associated with winning or losing, but it is about finding a way to create a total win-win situation.

A leader may go wrong sometimes, but he should be able to admit mistakes on his part. A leader today is not thought of as a person who solves all problems; rather he is looked upon as a person who helps others to deal with their problems and issues.

A good leader is the one who minutely evaluates situations and develops better ideas. To do this effectively, one has to keep some points in mind. If someone ends up telling about why a certain idea is bound to fail, think about the merits and demerits of that idea. This will help you analyze whether a certain situation can do without inclusion of that particular concept.

Negative impact can sometimes make us abandon fruitful opportunities. Try to think of the merits of an idea and how it can be used to achieve success.

Sometimes in gust of enthusiasm we tend to overlook the obstacles. This is a grave mistake and is usually the main reason behind the failure. Figure out the potential obstacles and configure a well-planned strategy to overcome them.

Best plan is to get all the work done in a distributive style. List all the necessary steps and the assign the task to specific or specialized persons.

Every difficulty presents you a unique opportunity. You can use it to your best advantage. Most aspiring leaders love to take up new challenges. But one should not get carried away by any stray or hovering difficulties. Ignorance or negligence can never help you get rid of prevalent pestering problems.

If you are able to look through the mist of difficulty, people will see it too. Such situations demand visionary leaders. The determination of a leader should not get fogged by difficulties or overwhelming situations.

Once you see your way through the difficulties it is relatively easy to boost the confidence of your teammates. This moral resurgence sometimes works wonders while accomplishing a task.

CHAPTER 2: TRAITS & CHARACTERISTICS OF LEADERSHIP

We come back again to the question "are leaders made or born?" Some people possess certain characteristics that come naturally to them when they are put in leadership positions.

With deliberate and well-planned efforts, one can learn the ropes of leadership. Exemplary character is essential for a leader. A leader should be trustworthy enough to lead other people.

Integrity and honesty on the part of a leader are essential for a successful implementation of leadership strategies. Leadership requires authority and it can only be gained through respect that is earned by trust.

You can motivate people for a cause only if you are really enthusiastic about it. People will respond to new ideas if they can feel the same passion as you about the task that has to be done. Inspiration and passion can be very contagious at times. You can't expect people to do certain things if you are not passionate about them in the first place.

It is true that the in terms of responsibilities a leader might seem as a different entity altogether, but a leader should always be seen as a part of the team. Goals can be achieved only through good comradeship. A leader should not be ashamed of doing any work that may look insignificant prima facie.

The power of confidence makes people believe in the idea that goals can be achieved in spite of all the obstacles. A leader has to be confident and bold at all times.

Confidence is also a contagious quality. If you are not sure about what are you doing, people tend to suspect your abilities. This may dampen the spirit of your team mates.

To promote best efforts from your teammates you should be able to clearly convey confidence to your teammates.

Order and purpose of job are of utmost important at all times. If you are sure about what are doing and how has to be accomplished, you can guide the people with sheer confidence. In circumstances of uncertainty this aspect of leadership can be of great help.

In dire situations, people look up to the leader and at such times this cognizance helps him reassure them about the success of the project. This gives a sense of security and self-assurance to them.

Calm and self-control are the much-needed assets required in a leader. In chaotic situations, he should be able to think clearly and steadfastly to fulfill purpose of task. This is the way you should lead, confidently.

Analytic thinking is another quality expected of a good leader. While you are focused on achieving a goal you should be able to analyze all types of circumstances to avoid any hindrance to the achievement of your goal.

As a leader, you should be committed to excellence. If you always compromise for the second-best position, this attitude will never lead you to success. Always strive for the best. A good leader always maintains high but achievable standards and raises the bar reasonably from time to time to achieve greater excellence.

All these characteristics culminate to produce the best leadership qualities in you. No person is born with all of these qualities. The key is to find the missing qualities and nurture them so that strong leadership traits can be developed.

CHAPTER 3: LEADERSHIP APPROACHES

There are various approaches that can prove to be very helpful to achieve the goals by motivating people and implementing your plans. These various approaches are different styles of leadership. If you blend all these styles as per your needs you can emerge as a good leader.

What characterizes the authoritarian or autocratic style of leadership is usually called as 'bossing the people around.' Without paying any heed to the advice given by the followers if you are pushing your way through then it is an example of authoritarian or autocratic leadership.

Authoritative style of leadership is quite helpful if you have all the necessary information or if you are running short of time. At such time one needs to delegate the task authoritatively. This style is not to be confused with the idea of yelling and threatening your followers with your power. It is certainly a malpractice to use your power and authority to abuse the team members.

This kind of leadership style should be used on rare occasions and that too with great care. You tend to lose your demeanor while applying this type of leadership.

The second and the most popular style of leadership is participative or democratic. As the name suggests this style of thinking allows the followers in the team to participate in decision making.

This style allows the participant to decide what to do and how it should be done. The decision making of course is done by the leader. Using this style of leadership is not at a sign of weakness but a strength.

This leadership style should be preferred when you do not have all the information needed to decide a plan. Your colleagues having the desired information can help you decide the best possible plan.

This style of leadership has twofold benefits it allows you work closely with your followers and at the same time helps maintain an amicable relationship with them.

This partial freedom is given in delegatory or free reign style of leadership. As a leader is unable to reach everywhere at all times this type of leadership becomes quite essential in some situations.

This style in no way allows you to blame your team for failure of a job. This style is to be used only when you have full confidence in your followers. Use it sparingly and wisely.

A good leader is one who uses all these styles with dexterity as situation demands.

While deciding which style should be applied a good leader takes into consideration points like how much time is on hand, the internal conflicts in group, the stress level, the type of work to be accomplished, how well informed the co-workers are and how much trust can be put into them.

CHAPTER 4: LEADERSHIP THEORIES

Leonard da Vinci once stated that a person who prefers to practice without theories can get lost on his path, just like a sailor who ventures out into the ocean without a rudder and a compass. There are eight principle theories regarding leadership. An aspiring leader must know a bit about all of them.

The first is the 'Great Man' Theory. This theory is based on the assumption that the leadership qualities are inherent and believes in the saying—Great leaders are born.

This theory paints a leader as mythic and heroic person and someone who is bound to reach the higher echelons of leadership. This leadership was considered strictly masculine and military sense.

Second theory is called as the Trait Theory. This theory too, believes that leadership qualities are intrinsic. This theory identifies with particular behavioral characteristics of a leader like adaptability, ambitiousness, cooperativeness, and some skills like diplomacy, fluency in speaking, creativity.

This theory fails to explain why some people fail to be good leaders despite the presence of the traits which are essential to be a good leader.

Next in the line is Contingency Theory. This theory focuses on some variables which are related to the environment that can determine which style of leadership is best in that situation.

The essence of this theory is that it states that no particular style of leadership is suitable for all the situations. The theory states that the success of leadership is dependent on a number of factors which may include the qualities of the comrades, the style of leadership and some varying circumstantial aspects.

Situational theory of leadership believes that a good leader chooses the best possible courses depending upon situations. The theory elaborates that choice of styles of leadership is affected by the situational variables. The appropriate choice of style of leadership can only be made by judging the intensity of the situation.

The fifth theory is the Behavioral Theory. This theory has a belief contrary to that of the 'Great Man' theory. This theory says that great leaders are not born but they are made.

This theory spotlights actions of a leader and do not pay unnecessary attention to the internal states and the mental qualities. This theory is deeply rooted in behaviorism.

The Participative Theory of leadership suggests an ideal leadership theory which takes opinions various other people into account. This theory promotes contribution and participation of team mates in the decision-making process.

It says that by doing so group members become committed to the task and feel more relevant for the task. It gives an impetus to their confidence but keeps the rights of decision making with leader at the same time.

The next theory is known as Management or Transactional theory. As the name suggests, this theory is based on the organization, supervision, and group performance.

The underlying guiding principle of this theory is reward and punishment. This theory is particularly used in business where employees are punished for failures and rewarded for success.

The last theory of leadership is the Relationship Theory. This is also known as Transformational Theory. It is clear as a day that this theory rests on the leader and follower relationship.

Leader helps group members to inspire and motivate them. This kind of leadership expects performance from each group member but also ensures that no team member gets exploited in this process. This leadership maintains high level of moral and ethical standards.

Leadership Models

To understand what are the reasons behind the acts of leaders one has to be aware of the various leadership models. It is better not to confine yourself into a specific behavior patterns explained in the ongoing discussion. The behavior should be in accordance with a particular situation.

The first model of leadership is the four-framework approach. As was suggested by Bolman and Deal, this leadership behavior has four types of frameworks viz. Structural, Symbolic, Human Resource, and Political. The correct choice is depends on the situation.

In Structural framework, the focus is put on strategy, structure, implementation, environment, adaptation and experimentation. This style focuses on analysis and design.

This framework is effective since goals of each section are clearly defined and they are technically strong. In this framework, the focus is on logic and task and not on emotions or personality. But if proven to be ineffective in some situations, this model seems to support tyranny that aims at focusing on petty details.

The Symbolic framework suggests a style of prophecy and inspiration. This model provides reasonable explanations of experiences. In case of ineffectiveness, fanaticism is associated with this model.

The Human Resources framework connotes that the leader is a catalyst. This is required to empower and support the team. The disadvantage of this framework is that the leader may become pushover.

The Political framework provides a strong linkage and bonding coalitions. The leaders have the power of clear assessment and equally clear expectations about the goals. The style may be somewhat manipulative or misleading.

The second model is Blake and Mouton Managerial grid. Simplicity is the key of attractiveness of this style.

High task and low relationship characterize the Authoritarian Leaders. These leaders are very much task oriented and may be a little hard on the followers.

They expect total obedience without questioning. They tend to blame the people rather than the wrong process. Quite intolerant by nature, these leaders are difficult to deal with.

Team Leaders are distinguished by their high tasks and high relationship traits. They are themselves exemplary and create an amicable environment helpful for better productivity.

They encourage teammates to achieve the goals effectively in optimal time. Such leaders are quite helpful to build an efficient and productive team.

Low task and high relationship are distinguishing features of a Country Club Leader. They are unable to maintain punitive and coercive powers which results in poor performance.

Impoverished Leader is the one who is low on task and low on relationship. They are not committed to task accomplishment or maintenance of the job. The team is allowed to do whatever they please.

The leader is detached from the team and there is no interaction whatsoever between the leader and the teammates.

⁇

.

CHAPTER 5: EXHIBITING LEADERSHIP

Exhibiting leadership may sometimes be confused with authority. This may have some negative impact on the attitude of your teammates towards you. To exhibit leadership without giving out airs of formal authority, is a tactful art. This art of exhibiting your leadership can be perfected with active efforts.

While exhibiting leadership you should keep some points in mind. Nowadays leader is not the one who 'leads' but is instead the facilitator who inspires others to achieve the desired goal. Coaching and motivation are two terms which are misunderstood.

A coach is a mentor and he usually dictates all methodologies and strategies. On the other hand, a leader is one who helps you decide to a better option.

Basics of the leadership have to be revisited if you want to know how to exhibit leadership in a positive manner. The pith of this entire thing is to indicate which direction to take and not to impose your followers to follow the dictated path.

The increasing complexity of tasks to be accomplished makes it impossible to reach everywhere all times. So, it is better to assign some small tasks to your co-workers.

This lightens your burden and makes the person working for you feel important which is beneficial to achieve certain goals.

Expecting leadership from the people at top is now outdated. In today's market oriented world, the leadership comes from the services and market focused products. It is a better idea to encourage leadership in prospective team members.

Believe it or not, appreciating others for their work is a sign of authority. You should not hesitate to compliment your seniors. A good environment helps to exhibit your leadership. Everyone wants a leader who can recognize the abilities of his followers. The due acknowledgement helps you to maintain a friendly relationship with all your subordinates and followers.

This ensures them that you are willing to work with them and not against them. This feeling of security fosters a much-needed friendly environment to increase their efficiency. If your co-workers are not feeling at ease to do certain duties, then your initiative can help them a lot.

This kind of initiative restores confidence in others and a way out of quandary can be found easily. This certainly helps people to accept you as a leader.

To be accepted as a natural leader you should change your conventional way of thinking. Consider everything that needs attention as your own responsibility in case no one is taking an initiative to do particular tasks.

This does not mean that you should be doing all the work by yourself. The only point is to keep things moving. If you take a negative approach that announces out loud 'This is none of my businesses!', no one is going to pay any attention to you.

A way to learn good leadership techniques is by trying to complete such types of work in a way that becomes an inspiration to others.

This naturally places you in the position of a leader. Doing a job in an organized way ensures the next task to be entrusted to you.

Lastly, do the job in such a way that it can facilitate your replacements, otherwise it will be deemed as bad leadership and no further such opportunities will be offered to you.

CHAPTER 6: HUMAN BEHAVIOR & LEADERSHIP

A leader has to interact with his followers along with those people whose support he needs to accomplish various jobs. This needs motivation, which in turn needs understanding of nature of human behavior.

People behave according to certain principles that govern their moods as well as work principles.

There are needs of a man which are physiological like water, food, sleep, and some are psychological like security, affection, self-esteem. Maslow hierarchically arranges these needs.

With increasing importance, the order is like physiological (food, shelter, water, sex), safety (freedom from danger), love (closeness to a friend), esteem (feeling of recognition), cognitive (learning and contributing knowledge), aesthetic (curiosity of inner workings of things), self-actualization (the state of well-being), self-transcendence (level that emphasizes intuition, unity consciousness etc).

Everyone tries to move up in the hierarchy but gets hindered by forces which are not in their control. A leader has to help these people acquire necessary skills that will push them on the hierarchy permanently.

Based on hierarchy of needs given by Maslow, Herzberg developed a list of factors which are termed as Herzberg's hygiene and motivational factors.

The factors like working conditions, admin policies, salary, supervision, status, job security, co-workers, and personal life are termed as hygiene or dissatisfies.

While the factors like recognition, achievement, advancement, growth, responsibility, and job challenges are called motivators or satisfiers.

How human behavior at work and organizational life is affected by opposing perceptions is depicted in theory X and theory Y. According to McGregor companies follow either of the theories.

Theory X assumes it is role of the management to control and coerce people. This theory says that the people have intrinsic dislike for work and try to avoid it if possible. People should be directed and coerced to achieve the objectives. People in general have little ambition, avoid responsibility and hence should be dictated.

This theory states that most people seek to give utmost priority to their own security.

Theory Y assumes that the management's role is to build up potential in employees and use it to accomplish the common goal. This theory believes that work is as natural as play. People implement self-direction if they are committed to an objective.

People can learn to seek and accept responsibility. People have capabilities to use their imagination and creativity to solve an organizational problem.

People have potential to shoulder the responsibilities. While a boss likes the X theory approach a leader mostly prefers the Y theory approach.

Clayton Alderfer's Existence/Relatedness/Growth (ERG) theory is based on a postulate which assumes that the needs can be categorized in three groups.

According to him the three categories are Existence, Relationship, and Growth. Most of the contemporary theories agree with him.

Vroom's expectancy theory is presented in a formula which is stated below.

Valence × Expectancy × Instrumentality = Motivation.

Valence is the amount of desire for goal, expectancy is strength of belief that works towards completion of work, and instrumentality is belief in reward which is received at the end of the work.

⍰

CHAPTER 7: LEADERSHIP & TEAM MANAGEMENT

Leadership and management are two different things which are used interchangeably. These two are totally different concepts. It is important to note that leadership is just one facet of management; there is a difference in perspectives of these two concepts. Manager rules while a leader leads.

First important thing to note while learning the differences between leadership and management is that leadership is just one aspect of management. Leadership is an important asset that is needed by a good manager. The aim of manager is to optimize the output and this he achieves through the administrative implementation.

To achieve this goal he needs organization, proper planning, and necessary staff, proper directing, and controlling. Manager needs a formal authority to be effective. Leadership is just one part of directing function. As self-motivated groups do not need leaders, it becomes evident that leadership is an asset, and not a requirement.

There is a subtle difference in perspectives of management and leadership. Leaders think radically while managers think incrementally. Management is about doing things right and leadership is about doing the right things.

Leaders follow their intuition while managers follow the policies of company they are working for. A leader may be emotional but manager needs to be practical.

In small groups, it is often observed that a manager does not emerge as a leader. A subordinate member with some specific talent most of the times, leads the group in proper direction.

He gives the strategies, vision, values, and goals which are guiding posts for the action. This emergence of subordinate as a leader might sometimes be a reason for conflicts in a group. Manager may feel offended and believe his authority to be endangered, if group looks towards leader.

Loyalty is one quality which pronounces the differences between a leader and a manager. Groups naturally are loyal to a leader than to a manager. This loyalty earned by a leader is because of responsibilities taken by him in certain areas.

These areas are taking blame when something goes awry, celebrating even minor accomplishments, and giving due credit to all teammates. Leader is sensitive to people and nurtures mutual confidence. These qualities may be lacking in some managers.

People naturally follow a leader on their own while manager is considered as person to be obeyed. The position of a manager is only because of the authority given by company. A leader may be lacking organizational skills but his vision has power to unite people.

Managers are usually persons specialized in certain field and can work their way up in the company. Manager has a good understanding of how each stratum of system works and has sound technical knowledge. A leader can be anyone from a novice to an experienced worker having newer ideas that can work better.

In a nutshell, to manage and to lead are two entirely different ways of organizing people. Management requires rational, formal methodology while leadership requires emotions and passions. There are many examples of excellent leaders who never made good managers. A leader should try to learn some of managerial skills.

Tactics & Strategies of Leadership

Consistent patterns of behavior govern the leadership styles. There are certain tactics that are exercised by a leader to influence the followers. There are in all eight fundamental tactics which are used by a leader while leading a group. These tactics are independent of the styles of leadership.

These eight tactics are Direction, Persuasion, Negotiation, Involvement, Indirection, Enlistment, Redirection, and Repudiation.

The Direction tactic is authoritarian. The leaders with authoritarian style normally exercise this tactic. In this case leader just orders his followers to do what he requires. The leader should have the power to give orders to his followers, only then can he use these tactics.

There are two possible situations in which this tactic can be used. One situation is when a leader has no time to apply other tactic. The second situation to go for this tactic is when doing so is good for the organization.

The Persuasion tactic is all about explaining and convincing the people to get the job done. It is about make them believe that what you want to be done is the right thing to do.

Remember that everyone has curiosity and right to know why he is doing a particular thing. This tactic works well when the people to be persuaded are in the same or higher position than that of the leader.

It needs reasons to lead the people this way. You should be able to supply reasons why a particular thing is to be done in a particular manner.

Another of the important tactics needed is Negotiation. This means influencing by way of settlement which is acceptable to both the leader and people.

This may involve comprising something. This tactic in needed in some circumstances and can prove to be very effective.

Next is Involvement tactic. This tactic is about involving people in what the leader wants to be done and make them adopt the same goal as he has. This induces commitment in them to attain the goal.

This is one of the most powerful tactics. If this tactic is used along with certain other tactics as per the need of hour, it can work wonders.

The involvement tactics give a feeling of ownership and people naturally work with fervor for things that they own.

In limited authority, a leader can use the Indirection tactic. This tactic is useful when people resist a direct influence.

In this tactic, the leader does not ask directly what he wants but he engages in some other task that will make people do the thing that he want them to do. When the direct approach fails, this is the best alternative tactic available for a leader.

In Enlistment Tactic, the leader just asks the followers to the desired thing. When the leader has no power or he do not want to use it this tactic is exercised.

The reason given to why a certain thing is to be done need not be logical or persuasive. If the real reason behind a certain action is not revealed then the leader is said to be using the redirection tactics. This tactic is used to avoid certain negative impacts. Giving reasons other than the true reasons is sometimes needed and is completely legitimate.

Disclaiming inability uses the Repudiation tactic to do the desired thing. The leader may have knowledge of how a certain task is to be accomplished but he denies his ability to do so. He then helps the person who has stuck doing the job. This way he leads the stuck person to learn a particular job and can get the job done at the same time.

The ever-changing situations require the leaders to use all these tactics in different point of time which of course depends the intensity of the situation. It is advisable to choose flexible leadership style with capabilities of using different tactics as per the need.

CHAPTER 8: LEADERSHIP DIRECTION

Surging waves of the river if left undirected can create havoc, taking lives of millions and rendering million others homeless-a total catastrophe, but if properly nurtured and rightly directed these waves can render any pasture green, bringing life everywhere.

Every soul dreams but few are able to realize those dreams and are able to give shape to their ideas whereas the all-powerful time devours the rest.

These few who make history, who influences millions of other souls and who keeps on pursuing their dreams in spite of all adversities are considered to be the leaders.

A leader is one who leads by example; he always sees light when others see darkness and he never loses hope. He knows what he wants, why he wants and how to achieve his wants.

To know what we want and to also know how to achieve these wants is not the same thing. Many great ideas start with much fanfare but do not reach its final destination due to lack of proper direction.

If a leader wants to move in the right direction then he should know how to plan his actions and be well aware of all do's and don'ts while pursuing our cherished goal. If you fail to plan, you plan to fail, each one of us our aware of this fact still none of us know how to properly plan.

While planning to identify all the requirements which will be essential to accomplish the objective, study all the pros and cons associated with the objective, and outline the difficulties which he will come across in the future while pursuing the objective.

A brainstorming and division of work needs to be done along with the proper allocation of resources. Allocate the work as per the talent and liking of an individual. If an individual gets the work of his choice then he will definitely do the work with extra enthusiasm and energy.

A leader does not try to do all the things in one go rather he defines all the tasks and decide which things to do first and which to do later. Draw a time table for each objective and try to achieve the objective as per the schedule.

In case of coming across problems, first identify the problem and then try to understand the causes which led to the problem. After completing a particular objective, check the performance to find out whether the requisite standard has been achieved or not.

In case the work being not up to the standard, suitable changes can be done. Now finally a leader just needs to act as per the plan. He always tries to build a team and allocate the work as per the member's talent and liking.

A leader should be able to properly lead his team by always giving the members the right direction, by always motivating them and by communicating properly with them.

Leadership and communication

Great ideas are lost, great missions fail and empires disintegrate when people are not able to properly communicate with each other. Communication is the most important tool, in fact, the only tool, which helps a leader to lead his followers towards the coveted goal.

Communication is the process by which a communicator is able to communicate the message to the audience and the audience is able to completely assimilate the original context.

In communication, there is a sender (the one who is delivering the message) and the receiver (to whom the message has been delivered). The message passes through an external environment.

Technically speaking, there are three processes to a communication viz. thought, encoding and decoding. First a thought or an idea generates in the mind, these thoughts and ideas are then encoded in verbal or textual form and these thoughts and ideas are finally decoded by the receiver.

If different receiver decodes the message differently, then the original texture takes a beating and everything looks hazy.

The message needs to be communicated in such a way that the receiver should be able to properly comprehend the actual meaning of the message.

Communication can be verbal or written. During verbal communication, apart from the words the audience also takes note of the communicator's tone of voice, his body language, his hand gestures and his overall attitude-these all constitutes non-verbal communication.

Having proper eye-contact with the audience gives an impression that the speaker is giving lots of importance to the audience. Use of simple words, words which penetrates deep into the heart of the audience, creates a lasting impression in the receivers' mind.

Proper variation in the tone of the voice as per the context of the message is very much desired; do not be too fast or too slow while speaking. Too fast a communication makes the audience misunderstand you, while if you are too slow then the audience will soon get bored and you will lose their attention.

While speaking, be warm, friendly and approachable; always carry an eye-catching smile on your face, speak lively, always use comfortable words, try to grab the attention of the audience by using some interesting quotes or phrases but never deviate from the original topic.

Communication is a two-way process; hence, feedback is an important ingredient of effective communication. The communicator should be earnest enough to know what actually the receiver feels about his message; and with all sincerity accept the verdict.

You might think you have used the best sentences, the best words, the best phrases but if the receiver fails to understand your 'best' then it's best to through your 'best' into the best dustbin.

There are certain barriers to communication which need to be taken into account; as its proper understanding may help the speaker to understand the audience in a much better way before he actually starts communicating.

Understanding the culture of the audience is of great importance, some gestures or some words may be unacceptable in certain culture.

Many times, the audiences carry some pre-conceived idea about something which needs to be dealt with very carefully. It is only through proper communication that a leader is able to effectively lead.

CHAPTER 9: TIME MANAGEMENT & CREATIVITY

A moment's life gone is gone forever; no amount of treasure can buy it back. Every individual rich or poor, young or old, men or women, white or black, irrespective of caste, creed and race, have got the same 24 hours per day in their life.

Those who are effectively able to use these 24 hours of theirs have the world at their feet while others fret and regret cursing the will of providence for their misfortune, little realizing that Lord Almighty played the fair game, but it was they who wasted time when their brethren toiled hard.

This precious gift of time should be used judiciously, in fact leaders are always very careful not to waste their time.

Irrespective of all the efforts we always find ourselves unable to handle the time to our advantage. Why is it so? Let us invest some time to understand how to effectively manage time.

Lack of proper planning of work is one of the major causes. Most of us indulge into an activity without analyzing its pros and cons; we do not interpret the problems associated with our action and just out of an instinct decide to go for it.

When struck with reality our lack of preparedness forces us to withdraw, thus a great amount of time is wasted without achieving anything.

Some of us love to procrastinate, while others love to get involve in thought provoking exercise such as lamenting about the past and hankering about the future, while others who think themselves to be too smart prefer to do all the activities on their own because they think delegating the work means compromising with the quality as they feel that they are gifted with supreme intelligence and all others are not up to their standards.

Leaders effectively manage time which is important so that the work is delegated. The goals are properly identified and broken down into long term, mid-term and short term; in fact, micro management of time smoothen our work.

Proper and realistic time table are made by a good leader, the priorities are well identified, and many tasks are handled at one time. This requires tremendous mental anxiety and the progress should be analyzed at regular intervals.

Creativity is the originality and the ability to do something which is completely new in this world; it is to think out of the box. In this ever-changing world, the thing which always seemed constant was creativity and thanks to creativity many fields today are still relevant.

Be it the field of science or technology or be it the field of arts or literature they survived because the creative leaders in these fields constantly bathed the humanity with new concepts and new ideas.

But in today's fast paced life when everything is measured in terms of profitability, people hesitate to experiment with new ideas for fear of failure, for fear of ridicule or for fear of losing their well-established career.

Leaders since time immemorial have used creative ideas to further their causes; these leaders wrote the history of mankind and were always desirous to welcome new ideas for the benefit of the whole humanity.

When Mahatma Gandhi gave out the concept of non-violence, the world was taken aback. A revolution without violence, this was something that none had ever dreamed, but this single idea gave a new dimension to the modern struggle for justice.

Leadership and creativity often complement each other. A leader should constantly evolve himself, he needs to constantly have innovative ideas; if he tries to survive on his old stereotypical image then it's just a matter of time when he will be inculcated into history.

A leader should also encourage creativity. Any creative idea finds acceptance if it is able to make significant contribution to a person's life.

Creative ideas can be in any field; it can be in the field of science and technology, it can be in the field of arts and literature, it can be in the field of music and theatre; in fact, creativity depends on how deep a person can think, the field is absolutely immaterial when associated with creativity.

At present, leaders in many organizations try to adopt the same old method of leadership fearing that the new ideas may not bring the desired results; they think the new ideas would result in wastage of time, money and valuable resources.

Such concerns are completely misplaced; because history has numerous examples wherein we can see that a particular organization which was once a leader have withered into oblivion because of their unwillingness to be creative.

Those industries that have been innovative and valued creativity have not only survived the onslaught of time but today have become a behemoth. This is why great business leaders always valued creativity and have always encouraged it.

Being able to take risks is worthwhile as it helps in survival. Not only in business but in politics too; great leaders have shed the stereotypical ideas and have brought revolution with their all powerful new ideas.

New ideas indeed face lots of resistance because they are unproven. Purist fear them and many think that implementing them is similar to digging their own graves.

It comes down on the leaders to motivate their followers to accept new ideas; a leader is one whom the people believe and trust, whom they think has the capability to help them realize their dreams. So, a leader should use their personal magnetism to spread hope and enthusiasm within their team.

CHAPTER 10: AFTER ACTION REVIEW IN LEADERSHIP

The difference between a leader and a statesman is that a leader after accomplishing any task jumps to the next task whereas a statesman after accomplishing a task reflects back to contemplate on the finished task.

A statesman wants to find out how the task was achieved, have all the objectives been accomplished and was there any scope of doing it in a much better manner.

After action review is very important in all most all the organizations, whether in politics, in military, in business, in sports and in many others. The leader is one whom others follow, but a leader cannot do all the work by himself he requires the assistance of others to reach to the final destination.

A review meeting after achieving a particular objective ensures that the mistakes won't be repeated again. A review meeting also helps to find out how the work could have been accomplished in a much better manner.

In today's fast paced life, it is not the hard work which matters the most instead it is the smart work which differentiates a winner from a loser.

 A review meeting should never become a blame game exercise wherein everyone tries to find a scapegoat. Focus of the meeting should be not to find a culprit but focus should be on the process which resulted in a particular outcome.

An open-minded approach should be adopted during the review meeting wherein other suggestions and opinions should be respected irrespective of their designation.

Free and fair discussions establish mutual trust among the employees; it enhances proper coordination among the employees and gives a feeling of self-worth to the employees.

The participants in the meetings should feel free to express themselves and the agenda to be discussed should be decided well in advance and no one should be allowed to deviate from the core theme.

Review meetings should be conducted in a friendly atmosphere and at the end of the meeting, something tangible should come into picture. After deciding the agenda of discussion in a review meeting, first discuss on the actions which were taken during the whole process.

The concerned person should provide an in-depth story. Analysis should be based on the detailed report wherein the participants should get into brainstorming to find out what went wrong which caused failure.

Or, if the outcome has been positive then find out whether there are any better measures which could have resulted in cost cutting or time cutting.

Try to find the reasons for the failure; the failure can result due to lack of proper coordination among the employees or due to unavailability of the resources, or due to time constraint.

Leaders should try to think critically and should remain completely unbiased during the whole process. Sometimes the outcome necessitates adopting some tough measures and the leaders should not shy away from it.

At the end of the whole process the leader should be able to understand other viewpoints and should come up with a viable solution which should be acceptable to all.

CHAPTER 11: LEADERSHIP STYLES

MOTIVATIONAL LEADERSHIP

Nothing is impossible unless you think feel it is. The difference between a loser and winner lies in their attitude towards their life and towards the goal which they were pursuing and their ability to motivate themselves in accomplishing the coveted goal. It is the lack of self-motivation in people which is a major cause of their failure.

A person may have all the important traits of a leader but if he is unable to motivate himself or others then it is very unlikely that he will be able to lead the team towards the final destination.

To accomplish a goal, we need others and these others will only be helpful if they are motivated enough to do the assigned task in an efficient manner. A leader should show extraordinary enthusiasm and commitment and should set an example for his subordinates.

His missions should be crystal clear, the steps required to achieve the mission should be properly laid down, the work should be properly delegated, and the expectations from his team members should be clearly communicated. It's hard work to polish a diamond to perfection; in fact, this is also true in case of dealing with the people.

Every individual is blessed with some great qualities and they also have something which most of us do not like. A leader knows this very well and he focuses only on those qualities of individuals that he requires; in fact, sometimes he is ready to tolerate someone's nuisance, if his priority is getting a certain work done.

One of biggest tragedy is that most of the individuals do not know what is bagged up in them; a leader delves deep into this unexplored area and inspires the individual to realize his true potential.

Effective communication is not just enough to motivate an individual; an environment should be created wherein an individual is able to motivate himself.

A leader should first try to understand the person with whom he is dealing with; understanding his emotions, his likings and his dislikes, building a good rapport with him and above all giving a feeling that 'I care for you' helps a leader to establish a heart-to-heart relationship with the person.

Once an emotional chord has been established it becomes a cakewalk for the leader to orient the individual in the direction he wants; the leader should always use the true potential of that individual as it would help in getting the work done with a much greater efficiency.

Actions always speak louder than the spoken words. So, a leader should lead by setting an example. Great leaders always did whatever they preached; they not only gave out advices, but also set up solid examples through their actions and deeds.

In any organization, it is important that the employees should be motivated by their leaders; the leader should properly delegate the work to his subordinates as per their talent and help them realize that their success lies in achieving the mission for which they have been working.

TRANSFORMATIONAL LEADERSHIP

Transformational leaders are very high in motivation and energy and their focus is not the short-term goals, in fact they are more inclined towards achieving higher goals. Here, though the leaders and followers can have different purposes in the beginning but more than often they try to fuse these purposes to pursue a much higher goal.

Transformational leaders might reflect some trait of charismatic leaders like being able to influence the people in an emotional way but they are different from charismatic leaders.

The transformational leaders display high risk-taking ability. Common people hesitate to take risk as they fear failure. High risk ensures high gain; these leaders are aware of this fact so they never hesitate in taking risk.

In fact, they are able to convince their followers to move ahead on his ideas, and his personal magnetism too ensures that the followers follow their leaders command.

They are excellent communicators; they are effectively able to establish a heart-to-heart relationship with their followers; the followers imbibe the message of their leaders and are able to cross that extra mile with great energy and extraordinary enthusiasm to fulfill the dreams of their leaders.

These leaders do not hesitate to recognize the efforts and contribution of their followers and are ready to appreciate them for their efforts. Transformational leaders are able to infuse a great amount of enthusiasm in their followers; their motivating gestures fill the atmosphere with lots of energy.

Their followers always appear self-confident and self-motivated. These leaders always look ahead and have a great vision; they guide their followers towards those visions. Slowly and steadily they develop a mass base; they keep their followers hooked to them by following what they preach.

They display great amount of personal integrity which makes them trustworthy. The followers start relating their own dreams with the dreams of their beloved leaders. They are very proactive and always lead from the front. They occupy the central position during their course of action and accept all the responsibilities.

These leaders are always accessible to their followers, and they are highly committed; in fact, their passion ignites even the young minds to follow them.

One of the negativity associated with the transformational leaders is that their energy and enthusiasm can also mislead the general masses which can be disastrous for the society.

Transformational leaders develop a vision and believe that they can transform their vision into reality but fail to analyze the efforts which would be required during the course of action.

Many of the followers who get inspired to join may soon find the vision unrealistic and unachievable; feeling cheated they would soon leave these leaders.

These leaders always want to transform the society but it's not always possible to bring a great change in the society; this causes a lot of frustration in these leaders.

However, despite of some shortcomings everyone would agree that we are indeed indebted to these transformational leaders for making constructive changes in the society and showing people the right path.

SITUATIONAL LEADERSHIP

Different situations need to be dealt in a different way; different people should also be dealt in diverse ways as well. Situational leadership theory states that a leader should not consider all the circumstances to be similar and apply the same methodology to deal with each one of them.

In fact, different styles are recommended for to deal with new situations in order to get the desired outputs.

Hersey and Blanchard gave a model on situational leadership which is highly acclaimed. They believed that the leaders should be very flexible and should be able to adjust themselves to the new situations and new circumstances very quickly. Leadership style and Development level are the two concepts on which their model is based.

Leadership style states that there are four categories of leaders viz. Directing Leaders, Coaching Leaders, Supporting Leaders and finally Delegating Leaders.

Directing leaders are those who lead from the front; they communicate the task to his subordinates and very closely examine the progress of the task. These leaders rarely discuss the ideas with their followers which are in contrast to Coaching Leaders.

Coaching leaders are very much open to suggestions and ideas from their subordinates and in fact they even implement those ideas. This kind of two-way communication helps the leader to develop a good rapport with their followers and is held in high esteem by their followers.

Though such type of leaders may look very attractive, but it might not be applicable in all situations. There are moments when the leader has to be tough; in fact, different situations warrant different styles.

In case of supporting leaders, it is the subordinates who have control over the decisions and the leaders just become a facilitator during the whole process.

On the other hand, the delegating leaders entrust the work to their subordinates; though the leaders are the part of the decision making but it is the prerogative of the subordinates to allow the leaders in the decision-making process or not.

The followers whom the leader leads, also has different traits and they exhibit different developmental levels. These developmental levels are: Low competence, Low commitment; Some competence, Low Commitment; High Competence, Variable commitment; High Competence, High commitment.

The followers have different levels of competence and their commitment for a given task too varies. Some followers may be highly skilled but may not exhibit great commitment about their work whereas others may be highly committed but may not have the requisite skill.

Some may fall in between i.e. they might exhibit moderate amount of commitment and moderate amount of skill.

A leader should know when to adapt and how to adapt because it is the leaders who need to transform themselves as per the demand of the situation and not the followers.

Depending on the developmental stage of the followers a leader will have to make his move; before taking any step, a leader need to also understand the psycho-physical nature of the follower. Overall, situational leadership demands that the leader to be versatile enough if he wants to get the desired results.

⍰

TRANSACTIONAL LEADERSHIP

Transactional leadership is based only one assumption that inculcates rewards and punishments as two important factors because of which an individual commits himself for a particular task.

When the task is accomplished as per the expectation then the doer is rewarded and if the result is not as per the expectations or if an individual fails to accomplish the task then he is punished for his failure.

Many argue that in this style, no importance is given to a person's emotional well-being and he is just thought to be motivated by reward which is monetary in almost all the cases.

The transactional leader clearly states what he actually wants from his subordinates; the subordinates also have the freedom to get themselves clarified before actually accepting the task.

In detail, the subordinate is told about the rewards which he would be getting after successfully completing his work. Though the punishments are generally not clearly stated but it is often understood by the subordinates.

He is provided with all the resources which he will require during the course of his work and is also trained in the initial period so that he gets an idea about his work.

Once he begins working, he is completely accountable for all his actions. Success or failure is his responsibility; his excuse of lack of time, or lack of resources or lack of proper support from his teammates is not generally entertained.

By accepting all the terms and conditions the subordinates also accept the full authority of the person under whom he is working. Management by exception (MBE) and contingent reward are considered to be the essential component of transactional leadership.

MBE mechanism ensures that the resource constraint should never become a cause of not achieving the desired result. Contingent reward means that a leader commits to the follower of rewarding him if he is able to provide the result. In fact, achievers are promised good rewards; rewards can be in the form of cash or it can be in the form of recognition.

In transactional leadership, the leader is often dominating and his main concern is to get the work done. The leader constantly keeps an eye on his subordinates and properly monitors him so that the subordinates do not deviate from the path.

In fact, a leader always wants that he should get the result in a specified period of time; failure of which irritates him which clearly reflects in the reward given to the subordinates. There are lots of critics to this style of leadership; rewards and punishments are not only the motivating factors as per them.

True indeed, emotions do play a very important role in a person's commitment towards the work. Negative emotions do hamper the work. However, it is a proven fact that rewards more than often, become the leading factor in motivating a person to work harder.

⍰

CHARISMATIC LEADERSHIP

What is charismatic leadership all about? It is the magnetic personality of the leader, which attracts peoples' mind, body and soul. These people willingly accept their leader's authority and are ready to lay down even their lives for the pleasure of their beloved master.

Mahatma Gandhi, who never even dressed gallantly, galvanized millions of Indians against the British and forced them to leave India. The revolutionary concept of non-violence was his sole weapon along with a tremendous mass appeal was his advantage over the British.

Alexander the great crossed the unconquerable Alps Mountain along with his soldiers, which until then no one had conquered. What was it that led their followers to believe in them that they did the unthinkable?

These leaders, charismatic indeed, had won the trust of their followers to such an extent that the followers believed in every word, in every action and in every deed of their leader.

Charismatic leadership is a trait and such leaders constantly hone their skills to win their followers' loyalty. Charismatic leaders constantly device strategies and keep on innovating themselves so that their followers are always with them.

Charismatic leaders first try to understand the environment in which they are working. They give lot of importance to peoples' moods and sentiments and try to associate with them personally. They exhibit tremendous and deep faith in their followers.

They enchant their followers' heart by their wit and charm. Charismatic leadership is not only about using words to impress the followers; it is also about conveying the right message to the followers with an effective body language.

Charismatic leadership is also about creating a unique identity of the group, which is very distinct from the other groups. The leaders create a distinct image of the group in the minds of the followers so that the followers can easily identify themselves with the group, which in turn gives the followers a sense of belonging.

The charismatic leader has tremendous self-belief; they always walk the talk, have patience and exhibit tremendous determination. They have high risk-taking capability.

They are ready to give up conventional ideas and willingly go for unconventional methods to achieve the desired result; most of the time they succeed with sheer excellence.

Not everything about charismatic leadership is fascinating. It has some darker sides too.

What if a charismatic leader starts believing that he is infallible? What if he starts using his charisma to ruin the young and tender minds? Leaders like Hitler, Stalin and more recently Bin Laden have used their charisma to fulfill their sinister motives and have created a chaos in the society.

These leaders sometimes become addicted to glorification and are unable tolerate any kind of criticism. They generally refrain from grooming others for leadership, as they do not want anyone to question their authority.

In spite of some ill effects, a charismatic leader not only transforms the society but also provides a new meaning to human civilization. Martin Luther King, Mahatma Gandhi, Swami Prabhupad - the founder of ISKCON, Margaret Thatcher, Abraham Lincoln, Malcolm X were some of the charismatic leaders who have defied many odds and have brought about radical changes in the society.

⍰

ETHICAL LEADERSHIP

Ethnic and communal hatred is today one of the major causes of concern. Today in the name of caste, creed and religion people kill each other. Today's leaders often spread hatred among various communities in order to protect themselves as a champion of a particular community.

This can lead to very dangerous situations. Leaders are people who have the capability to galvanize people for some specific purpose. If the purpose is constructive, it creates a just society wherein people live together happily in complete peace and harmony but if the leader has got some sinister motives then it would bring mayhem in the society.

Today ethics, which have lost its sheen among the leaders, need to be promoted.

Let us understand what actually ethical leadership is. Ethical leadership is about having certain standards and principles. Here a leader just does not lead but he always monitors his activity seeing whether he is keeping up the standards or is he deviating from the set standards.

He will be ready to suffer loss but will never be ready to compromise with his principles. Today it is very much required in the corporate world. Today companies hide their actual financial position to lure the investors. So, it is imperative that ethical leadership should gain momentum in the corporate world.

Communication should not just serve as a means for conveying a message but the communication should be ethical also. Enron of USA cheated the public by not disclosing their actual financial position. So, it is important that the industries should always state what is right though it might be bitter. Political leaders too should refrain from hurting the sentiments of other communities. They should promote tolerance among various communities.

Leadership also means giving the best to the public. In business, it is not just the shareholders and customers who should be taken care of but the business should focus on entire society including the biosphere.

Ethics demand that customers should get product of best quality at appropriate rate and there should be no alteration in it. Motive should not be only profit but the motive should also be to serve the customers.

Corporate social responsibility is today being practiced by most of the organizations. Here the companies use their capital for some social causes such as for child education, AIDS rehabilitation etc. It is a good practice and even the government is encouraging it.

Ethical leadership also demands that leaders, whether they are from industry or from other sectors, should have a broader outlook. They should not surround themselves with sycophants and take decisions based on their advice.

Leaders should have a proper succession planning wherein the other people are groomed as leaders so that they can take the charge once the incumbent departs. This prevents the void, which often creates havoc in any organization. Leaders should also occupy the office for a particular tenure after which they should voluntarily step out paving way for others.

Such practices in the political as well as corporate world will help in creating a better environment where people will live together without any hatred.

Leadership in Diversity

It is the people who are the building block of any organization; it is they who actually make the organization run. A leader can provide the vision, by giving new ideas, concepts and can delegate the work but it is the people who actually work.

No two people are same. Some are Christians, some are Jewish; some are black and some are white, some are western and some are eastern, some are young and some are old, there are males and also there are females, there are people who are extrovert and there are people who are introvert; there are fast learner and there are slow learners; some are dominating by nature whereas others are friendly, some are emotionally strong whereas others are too emotional by nature. It's a never-ending list!

Establishing proper coordination among all these people is too difficult; it's rather a Herculean task for any leader to build a team where each people get along well with each other.

People due to their pre-conceived notions, hesitate to interact with other people; they develop a stereotypical image of others in their mind and judge all the people as per their belief; they often feel uncomfortable in dealing with them.

The moment an individual enters an organization he starts searching like-minded people and confines himself to that group. This is very dangerous for any organization's future growth prospect.

A leader's role becomes very critical here as he is the one who can help these people to come together to work. He needs to communicate that each one of them is priceless but they have to work together with others to achieve the coveted goal.

This can be achieved by changing the attitude of an individual. This attitude which is generally developed during the childhood, or results because of some unique experience becomes a tool by which some individual starts judging other person.

This mindset needs to be changed by constant training and education. A leader should train the subordinates to give priority to the organizational objectives which can be realized if every individual works together. Efforts should be there on team building.

A team requires diverse people because diversity in the team will ensure that different people of different background will have different ideas which ensure a better idea.

A leader himself should not be biased; in fact, he should exhibit open-mindedness in accepting all the members of the team. He should exhibit his open-mindedness no just by words but by his actions also.

Working in diversity ensures capitalizing on the talent of each and every individual of the organization; this will provide competitive advantage to the organization.

This will also ensure that the members can learn from each other as everyone is blessed with some unique quality. Working in proper coordination ensures efficient work.

Communication can prove to be highly effective in enhancing relationships among the members; communication also plays great role in clearing any misunderstanding; it also helps people to change their pre-conceived mindset about an individual.

So, a leader should promote constant and regular communication among the employees. Once people open to each other it becomes easier to understand others culture and others way of living; the barriers may soon will lose its relevance and an atmosphere of love and mutual understanding will emerge wherein every people will respect each other and will work together towards a common goal.

VISIONARY LEADERSHIP

Shooting guns without knowing the actual target, kicking the ball without knowing the goalpost, a ship in the middle of the ocean without knowing which direction to go; these are all futile acts which will never bear any result.

Similarly, a leader without any vision leads his followers to nowhere; such leaders lead a purposeless life and their followers ruin their lives because they just keep on floating like a rock in the midst of the ocean, constantly being tossed up and tossed down by the waves of time.

A leader can only lead if he has immensely clear vision, a leader can only command the respect of his followers if he has a mission, and a leader can only win followers if he displays tremendous determination towards the achievement of the goal.

The vision needs to be clearly articulated to the followers; the followers should clearly understand the leader's message. Before embarking on any path, a follower should now what he is doing, why he is doing and finally by his act where he is going to reach at the end of the day.

 Understanding all this, infuses enthusiasm in an individual and he marches forward with utmost enthusiasm, courage and determination.

A leader needs to clearly set the organizational goal and organizational objectives. He should see that all the members are whole-heartedly involved in the process; if not he should try to motivate his followers by making them realize that the fulfillment of organizational objective will play a great role in their personal success.

The leader should lay great emphasis on team building; proper coordination among the members is very much required. The leader should infuse self-confidence in his followers and make them to visualize the bigger picture; the members should feel that they have become a part of something great fulfillment of which may bring a lasting change in the society.

Leader's team members will belong to diverse culture and will have different mind-sets; it is the leader's responsibility to use the unique talent of each member for the organizational goal and also promote coordination among all the members.

Leaders should not preach only by making use of his ever-powerful words, but his words should also match his deeds. He should become a living example for his followers. He should not just be a fantastic communicator; he should also be an excellent motivator.

His words should reflect his determination towards his vision while his actions should demonstrate his seriousness towards the mission. A positive environment of mutual understanding, mutual trust and mutual cooperation should be created.

A leader should also clearly define the set of activities which need to be followed during the course of action. Every member should know what actually he has to so, proper resource allocation is a must and time frame has to be set up towards the realization of each objective.

At each and every step a checklist should be there wherein the group can review whether they are moving in the right direction or whether they are treading on a wrong path; they can also mediate on the steps which can improve their performance. A visionary leadership provides the right direction and the right motivation.

CHAPTER 12: LEADERSHIP RELATIONSHIP

A person might be blessed with extraordinary talents; he might be the best orator or the best writer or the best in his field still he may not emerge out to be a great leader. People may possess almost all the traits of a leader, but if they lack the all-important human touch than they will fail to attract people towards themselves.

Leadership is about having great relationship with others; a follower is ever desirous of seeking personal association of his beloved leader. If a leader does not display the personal bonding then it's just a matter of time that the followers will abandon him.

A person is not compelled to follow somebody; instead he chooses to follow somebody. But why does he choose to follow an individual? What did he see in that particular individual that he decided to be dictated by his terms and conditions?

He submissively accepts an individual as the architecture of his destiny because he sees a personal touch in that individual's gesture, he sees someone who is showing great concern for his personal well-being and he sees that this individual is ever desirous of his success and is willing to provide him the necessary direction which can lead him to succeed. So, he decides to accept his authority and he becomes his follower.

A leader has to be credible and trustworthy. His words and actions should match; he should become a living example to his followers. Whatever expectations a leader has from his followers he should clearly state it.

People want a leader to be honest; a follower has willingly surrendered himself to the leader so he wants that the person whom he is following should be honest in his words and in his actions. A leader should be a great communicator of ideas and visions; his words should establish a bond with the follower.

A leader should create a positive environment wherein the people can be self-motivated; a leader should always be inspiring. He should display great amount of competence and commitment towards his work. He should lead by example and display tremendous determination; his never to die attitude will inspire his followers.

A leader should also display great competence and capability. People follow someone if they believe that the person has got the requisite capability of achieving what he tends to achieve.

Great leaders have always been people oriented rather than task oriented. These leaders willingly take accountability of others life; whether success or failure they ensure that their follower keeps on moving and remain motivated. Such display of concern infuses a sense of security in the followers convincing them that their lives mission can only be accomplished by completely surrendering to the will of the master.

The leader needs to articulate the goal and the ways by which he expects to achieve the goal. In pursuing the goal, he need to build a team; a team should consist of people of diverse background as it would help in brainstorming a unique idea. He should also promote mutual understanding, mutual cooperation and mutual trust among the members.

This can be achieved by having great relationship with every member without displaying any bias; the members will club together around the leader and will willingly accept to cooperate for their beloved leader.

CHAPTER 13: FOLLOWERS OR SUBORDINATES?

Although both the terminology-followers and subordinates- are often used (or misused) interchangeably still there are considerable differences between the two.

A manager manages the subordinates whereas a leader has followers who are ever desirous of pleasing their beloved leaders. The word 'beloved' may not go well with managers because subordinates do not willingly surrender rather they surrender out of some external motivation.

Followers and subordinates both work under somebody, but they are treated differently by their leaders. The way a leader handles a problem may be completely different than the way a manager looks at a problem.

A leader leads the mass; he wants people who are ready to assist him in fulfilling his vision; so, a leader desires a long-term association with his followers.

A manager is generally task oriented; he is more concerned about the successful completion of the task whereas a leader owing to long term objectives is not only interested in the completion of a particular task.

Managers display authority on account of their position in the company. This style of leadership which a manager follows is transactional in nature. Rewards and punishment are the two important constituents of this style of leadership.

A subordinate is promised a reward on the successful completion of a task; the reward is generally monetary in nature. Upon failure, he is liable to be punished, the punishment can be severe to milder in nature.

He can even lose his job if his performance is not up to the mark or he can be demoted from his position. Managers are generally averse of taking risk as his main focus is getting the job done as was desired. He generally refrains from adopting new ideas and new concepts.

Leaders due to their personal magnetism often attract people and these people whole-heartedly accept the authority of the leaders. Whether the leaders are charismatic or transformational they always pursue a higher goal and in doing so they require people.

They display a great amount of sensitivity and chivalry. The followers start seeking great pleasure in the association of their beloved leaders. The leaders are high on taking risks and more often comes up with new ideas and new concepts.

These leaders have the capability to convince their followers that the vision defined by them is not only achievable but will also help them to realize their personal objectives.

Followers always have a feeling that they are the part of some great mission and the success of the mission is instrumental in bringing radical changes in the society whereas the subordinates only concentrate on their task and their main motive to complete the task lies in the desire of getting rewarded.

Sometimes the followers trail a leader blindly as they believe the words of their leaders to be the Absolute truth. Whilst a subordinate before embarking upon any new task meditate thoroughly upon the benefits associated with the task. A leader rules the heart of his subordinate whereas a manager rules the mind of his subordinate.

Pillars of Leadership

There are many principles which guide a leader to gain trust of his followers. These simple principles are quite essential for successful leadership.

First of all, a leader must be present during the time of crisis. This visibility creates a sense of trust in leader. He must be able to take stand based on the vision and values that guide us to achieve our goal.

A leader should be engaged physically, emotionally, spiritually, and mentally in the task to be completed. He should be able to build social capital from a diverse network.

A leader should be able to overcome the overriding cynicism. He as a leader should be able to reaches extreme boundaries of innovation. One needs to be sympathetic towards his coworkers. An aspiring leader has to be capable of building a sense of community in group.

A leader should always strive for improvement. Last but not least, a leader should have a plan which will work towards the achievement of goal.

The resource management is one of the challenging tasks of a leader. If you fail to manage whatever resources you have you may end into difficulties.

First thing about management of resources is to identify the resources. If you can locate the resources correctly they can be used effectively as per the need of situation.

The second singular task about resource management is to determine where these resources are. This helps you to quicker organization of these resources at the time of need. It is also important to note how these resources can be obtained with least hassle.

The availability of resources does not ensure your success. What you need is a plan that can utilize the resources effectively. The manner in which you use your resources is also very important. You should be able to strike a balance while using these resources to the optimum level.

Resource allocation, strategic planning, and effective utilization of available resources are the factors that contribute to successful resource management.

CHAPTER 14: LEADERSHIP VS MANAGEMENT

Is there any difference between leadership and management? Yes, these two are totally different concepts.

The main difference between leadership and management is the way they motivate the people. Managers use the authoritarian style of influence whereas leaders have the transformational or charismatic style of influence.

Managers work for the money they get; they get the job done from their subordinates. The focus of leader is people. He should be able to motivate people to get the job done.

Managers are generally avoiding risks and try to avoid the arising conflicts. Leaders on the other hand are open to take risks and try different ways to get the task done. Managers have objectives and a leader has vision.

Managers are dependent upon their subordinates but leaders have their followers. This is one of the distinguishing factors between a leader and a manager. Management have authority to get the people work for them while a leader has the passion and motivating power which helps him to get the job done.

Common Misconceptions Between Authority & Leadership

The most common misconception about the leadership is that leadership is always based upon authority. Actually, the concept of a leader depends upon how we choose to define leadership. This in essence is taking charge of group to complete a task, without formal authority.

The concept of leadership of today has changed radically. This leadership may be called as informal leadership. This leadership has no formal authoritative position.

This may even escape formal acknowledgement of leadership by the group. The matter is quite unassuming. This is done subconsciously sometimes and only an outsider can observe that certain person is leading the group without slightest awareness on the part of group which is being led by him.

This informal leadership is simply being in charge on temporary basis. The leader is the person who guides the direction. He may take decisions and can influence people as a conventional leader.

They have only informal authority and these leaders use personal expertise, personal magnetism, and extremely powerful persuasive skills. They do not have authority but have strong force of will that make them appear an authoritative person.

The second misconception about leadership is that leadership is equivalent to management. As a matter of fact, leadership is an occasional act rather than an unending role.

Leadership is quite instantaneous, like a creative activity. For a good leadership, you need only good persuasive skill to make people follow the direction you want. This view clarifies the fact that anyone can show occasional leadership.

Leader is a godfather, is yet another common misconception. This conventional outlook has changed over the years. In an age of empowerment and knowledge every employee is needed to show informal leadership from time to time.

Another of prevalent misconceptions about leadership is that the leaders are born. This is not true at all. Many people who are not willing to lead give this lame excuse.

It is true that some people have certain qualities needed for a good leadership but is does not mean that those qualities cannot be acquired with some efforts. All of us can grow up and become good leaders. Leadership skill can be learned if you really want to be a leader.

Yet another misconception about leadership is that you have to be a superhuman being to be a leader. This also is not true. Many leaders are also normal average human beings like all of us.

The only thing is to make deliberate efforts which are needed for good leadership. You are bound to make certain mistakes while trying to be a leader but it is natural. Just think about your committed mistakes and try to avoid their recurrence.

Bosses represent authority and are sometimes confused with leaders. Remember certain subtle differences that distinguish a boss from a leader. A boss generates fear while leader creates confidence.

Boss spawns resentment while leader generates enthusiasm among the team members. Boss will always say "I", while leader will say "We".

A boss fixes blames faults of others and a leader helps to fix faults. Boss knows how to do and leader shows how to do. Under boss work is toil and under a leader work is fun. A boss drives and a leader leads.

CHAPTER 15: EVOLUTION OF LEADERSHIP

Leadership has been evolving over the years. This shift has been from leaders to leaderships.

To evolve leadership, on has to adapt and maintain opposing forces in group. This maintenance encourages efficiency, cohesion and consistency in the group. The group stability is disrupted by the adaptations but this instability is better than extinction.

These adaptations are done only when there are variations which are caused by people doing different things. Some of these variations are considered as deviances and some are called as leaderships.

Leadership is essentially a variation which leads the group to change the undertaken direction. The successful teams or groups are only formed by constant variations which need a good leadership.

When there is intense competition between the groups this speeds up the evolution of leadership provided that there is sufficient variation. Management is usually equated with maintenance. Managers get thing under way efficiently. They coordinate efforts of other people to get things done.

Leadership is an instrumental force that works for change; it is the driving force behind evolution. Leaders are those deviants with new ideas that augment the chances of success for a group.

A person who is in charge of the group may not be the only resource of variation. It is seen that the groups that do not allow more than one leader always reduce the potential amount of variation thereby limiting itself to few ideas only.

There are two motivating factors for those who want to lead. The first is to differentiate oneself by doing something different. This is the true basis of leadership. The second motivating force is to gain power over other people and to make oneself the only source of variation.

It is observed that those who are in power always want to suppress other variations. This is usually driven by the desire to hold the power. In modern organizations, this may not be done intentionally.

Some people are strongly oriented to acquire power while some people need protection from someone powerful. This can create high expectations which may be hard to meet in fast changing and complex environment.

This is the reason why the conventional leadership has proved counterproductive in today's world and hence, has been replaced by informal leadership.

Certain measures are to be taken to mend this. First thing is to note that is insufficient to advance leadership throughout the organization on by those in charge. All people in the organization need to take responsibilities. They should take initiatives on their own and rely less on leaders which are formally appointed.

In old days, attainment of power over other people was an affair of just strength. Then the authority was institutionalized. For ages and ages people are progressing from formal authority to the power of knowledge. Now the innovative or creational ability is not supposed as the monopoly of topmost people in the organization. The faculty now occurs at all levels especially at the frontline.

This new era leadership is not yet widely accepted or acknowledged. It will take some time but is bound to succeed in near future.

The roles of leadership have been changing over the years. The demands of roles of the contemporary leadership have changes considerably. For an aspiring leader, it is important to note these subtle differences in the roles of conventional and contemporary leaderships.

The leadership in old times was confused with the concept of management. But as we know these two are different concepts. Leadership is just one part of the management. The first difference between management and leadership is that of authority.

In old days, it was considered necessary to have authority to be a leader. This concept is now treated as outdated. For leadership, there is no need of authority. Leadership nowadays is just an agency through which new directions are explored.

In recent years, the strategic choices were considered as a realm exclusive to those in authority. This concept has also been changed. Now a leader can make decisive choices if the need arises. Such freedom is needed to have more chances of getting success at the earliest.

In those days, the leaders were little or not at all participative. This attitude puts a barrier between the leader and the workers and results in hampering the performance. This also alienates the leader from the entire group. This attitude is also changed in past years.

Participation of a leader in the effort to accomplish a certain task helps the leader to communicate with the group properly which is important for unity and understanding in the group.

Now a leader is supposed to interact even with the people who do not report to him directly. This helps to coordinate the job effectively and helps to foster the feelings of friendship.

The old basis of leadership was purely on power. The power to dominate people was supposed to be the sole requirement to become a leader. This notion also has undergone a drastic change in past years.

Now power to dominate is not at considered a quality to become a good leader. In today's knowledge-driven world power also has acquired a new meaning. The promotion skill and innovative ideas that lead to success are required to complete a job effectively.

These ideas can be provided by anyone who has brains. He can become a leader on these assets. A specialized knowledge about the job to be done is sufficient to raise you to the echelons of leadership. A person with such knowledge is looked at as natural leader in such cases.

In old days leadership was considered as a post to be held now it is a spontaneous activity. This too helps to achieve the goals as changing leadership is helpful to generate newer ideas. This has broken the monotonic nature of leadership.

The new age leadership is all about challenging the status quo. Anyone who challenges the conventional processes and can suggest better ways of accomplishing tasks is welcomed as a leader.

The conventional leadership was very much focused on the power and new age leadership is focused on novelty and creativity. According to new definitions leadership is not about bossing the people around; rather it is helping our teammates to achieve the common goal effectively.

CHAPTER 16: ARE LEADERS BORN OR MADE?

The debate of Born Leader versus Made Leader has been going on for centuries. This debate still continues but we now know that both the sides are partially correct.

The only thing a person must to have in order to become a leader is intelligence. He must also be smart enough. We know that leaders may not be the smartest people in group but he should be able to get the assigned job done. People usually grow up with certain characteristic and these characteristics matter in case of leadership.

A grown-up person can help other people to achieve goals. This is what a leader is supposed to do. They are supposed to help their subordinates evolve and develop. These are some qualities which are sometimes inborn in some people. Stern and intrinsic will formulate a group which is required by a leader.

Some people have a natural ability which makes them take initiatives in leadership. The will to make decisions is also one trait which is inherent in some people and proves to be an essential quality of a leader.

While some qualities needed for good leadership may be natural to some people it is important to note that all skills needed for leadership are not present in any individual. He has to learn some skill on his own by making deliberate efforts.

Since all the properties needed for good leadership are not inborn in any individual everyone has learn the ropes of this business. That is why it is stressed that leaders are made and are not born.

Anyone willing to become a leader can learn the basics of leadership. But in the gist of all this is that all the leadership cannot be taught in the actual sense.

Mainly leadership is learned through apprenticeship, an estimated 80 percent of leadership stuff is learned while doing the leadership job. To watch and to imitate leaders helps a lot. Aspiring leaders choose their role models and find their own mentors.

Mentors can also help resolve situations. The improvement of a leader always happens through the feedback and its analysis. This feedback is usually sought from subordinates, peers, and bosses.

They alter their behavior as per the feedback. All these things are to be learned and cannot be inherent in any person.

Trying different things out and then criticizing the performance is one way to learn ways of good leadership. This attribute is never intrinsic and has to be learned. No one is born as leader. Some of inborn traits can be potential material to become a good leader.

Only right stimuli are needed to become a good leader in such cases. Whether a person born with leadership qualities will become a leader or not greatly depends on the circumstances. If he does not get proper stimulus he will not become a leader in spite of his inbuilt qualities.

On the other hand, a person willing to become a leader can attain his/her goal by learning the skills needed and cultivating the qualities that are essential to become a good leader.

SUMMARY

Leadership is nothing but the art of persuading people to achieve organizational and individual goals by offering then the purpose of doing so, the proper direction, and most important of all the motivation to do it.

This is a process of working with a group to achieve a common goal. To do this one has to gain some skills because some skills and qualities that are needed for a good leadership are not inborn in any man. These qualities have to be cultivated. It is important to note that the statement 'leaders are born' is partially true and one has to work to perfect oneself as a leader.

There are various leadership styles like autocratic, democratic, and free reign no one having special advantage over the other. A good leader blends all these style as per the need of situation.

There are various leadership theories that categorize the types of leadership. Similarly, there are leadership models also. These models are based upon various frameworks like Symbolic, Human Resource, and Political.

Exhibiting leadership is an art. A wrong message should not be sent to the group members. People may confuse leadership with bossing which can have adverse effect on working.

As modern theory suggests leader is not to be confused with a boss, on the contrary he is the person who helps the group to achieve the common goal effectively.

The human behavior is the most complex thing to understand and a leader should have working knowledge of it. It helps him to understand the people's reaction to the actions taken. This understanding plays a decisive role while deciding strategy.

Good communication is an essential quality of leader. This enables better understanding between teammates. To understand the teammates and to be understood by them is quite necessary to lead a group.

Unlike the conventional leadership, modern leadership is based on the power of knowledge. Today a person need not have authority to become a leader.

What is needed in this knowledge driven complex world is creativity and the boldness to challenge the conventional ways of doing things.

Leadership thrives on motivation and for motivation a leader himself must be passionate about the work team is supposed to do.

Various kinds of leadership have evolved in recent years like motivational leadership, transformational leadership, situational leadership, transactional leadership, charismatic leadership, and ethical leadership.

For a good leadership, one has to maintain good relationship with his followers. You need a vision to accomplish the task. There is subtle difference between the followers and subordinates but you can learn to differentiate between them.

As a good leader, you should be utilizing your resources smartly. But this does not mean that leadership is nothing but management. Remember that these two are distinct concepts.

Over the years the leadership has evolved from leaders to leadership. It was person centered in the past and it has now evolved as activity centered.

The debate of 'nature versus nurture' has been going for the years but now it is an established fact that leaders are made and not born. Anyone with a will to become a leader can learn the skills of leadership.

There are various helping factors like exercise to develop leadership skills, various journals, mentors, peers, leadership coaches, and seminars available on the scene to help you.

Great leaders have come and gone. Their lives are example of the tradition of great leadership.

APPENDIX 1: LEADERSHIP EXERCISES & COACHING

There are many exercises that can help you develop excellent leadership skills. First of all, you should have a clear idea of what is meant by leadership. This is your starting exercise to contemplate upon what is meant by a good leadership.

This can be achieved by discussions and feedback. Once you get a clear idea of leadership you can work towards building a good leadership. Try to put what are your conceptions about leadership and then agree on a working definition.

Since there are various leadership styles, you can discuss advantages and disadvantages of these styles. This can help you gain a better understanding of when to use a particular style.

This discussion should include how the group reacts to particular styles of leadership. This discussion should guide you to infer that flexibility is necessary while using these styles of leadership.

The motivating exercises help you gain an insight in the situations and practices that motivates group members. Another activity that can be practiced is to see what effects are observed on the group when a new leader takes over.

What are the problems of the leader who takes charge of the group? What should be the approach towards a new joiner in a group is also an exercise. What should be a leader's attitude towards him is also an important factor of leadership.

Change implementation exercise helps you understand how the members of group behave if certain restructuring is done. One can learn about strategies regarding the problems that arise from such restructuring.

Clarifying objectives of the task has been the key to success. In this activity, you ask someone to note down proceeding of exercise where you clarify the objectives of the task to be done.

The feedback given by the person who notes the proceeding helps a lot to understand the benefits of clarifying objectives to group.

Clear communication exercises involve accomplishing something which is bound to fail if you do not communicate properly. This activity decides where you stand with respect to your communication skills.

The mapping leadership skill is an exercise to check how well you manage to succeed with given resources. The activity is so designed that good management of resources is needed for success. This assesses the how you can map your leadership skills.

Exercises designed for creative leadership is most rewarding. In these activities, a group leader has to guide the group for successful outcome. The observers then provide feedback which is priceless. This gives you an idea where you fall short while leading a group.

The delegating and monitoring is the soul of leadership. This activity hinges on successful monitoring, organization and delegation of tasks.

This team timed, exercise helps you to learn how a task can be completed within given time limit. On the other hand, speed delegation activity checks, how efficiently you can work against the clock.

There are more tasks to be completed with a fewer resources. The key is to plan your resources in such way that the task is completed within time.

In the routes to solution exercise, the teammates have bits of information and the leader has to link those bits and organize activity to achieve the goal.

Viewing the option activity hone your skills to use schedule the activities effectively. The budget for success exercise can be helpful to plan your activities within budget.

Leadership Coaching

As discussed earlier leaders are made and not born. As all the qualities for good leadership are not inborn in a person we need to learn some skills and qualities on our own.

Hence, coaching is needed to cultivate good leadership skills. There are various programs available that can help you acquire the skill which are needed to make a good leader out of you. Coaching sessions can be availed from your peers, specialized institutions or from self-help journals.

Now that we know coaching is needed for good leadership. First of all, you need to understand what is meant by leadership coaching. This is necessarily means a one to one relation with the coach who assists you to learn certain actions that are needed to reach the goal.

These coaches are experts in personal changes which are necessary to carve out the leader in you. They induce some changes in you which eventually help to fulfill your goal. They are professionals that train you in unique leadership skill. They are helpful in identifying your goals and prioritizing your actions and plans.

All the things needed to overcome the barriers, are taught to you by them. For learning the characteristics of a leader in systematic and methodic way, a leadership coach is probably the most suitable person.

Leadership coaching if clearly focused on the sustainable changes in the arena of influence. It is all about how you influence people to get the job done. The job of a leadership coaching is to help you learn these invaluable skills. There are various integrated methods applied to help you learn the leadership abilities. These methods include one to one method, tele-classes, workshops, peer guidance, and learning community. All these tools are meant to enhance the leadership qualities in you. The programs are custom made as per your requirements.

Leadership coaching is all about the leveling of playing field. This type of coaching is of two-levels. It may be team coaching or individual coaching.

Team coaching helps people to work together. Individual coaching is about situational leadership. This is one to one coaching which ensures good performance as a leader. This aims at increasing competence with the help of planning and professional guidance.

Coaching is important to develop higher commitments to the common goals to be achieved. The leadership coaching focuses on the balance of long term goals and vision of the organization. This fusion of personal goals with those of the organization is needed for leadership. A leadership coach stresses this.

Coaching is needed to produce valuable leaders. This may not be always a person. There are many good books and journals which can help you learn a thing or two about good leadership qualities.

These self-help type books are available in market. One who is studious and aspire to become a good leader can learn many things from these books. But be aware that understanding the principle or practices of leadership alone do not ascertain your success to become a good leader.

Leadership can only be learned through practice and experience. You should always keep in the mind that the coach and journals may teach you the nuances of leadership but success comes only through patience and self-help.

APPENDIX 2: LEADERSHIP JOURNALS & SEMINARS

There are some skills have to be learned for a good leadership. In some people, these qualities are inborn but some people have to learn these skills.

What are the means to learn these skills?

Either you can watch a leader and learn from him. The other way is to learn the skills is from a leadership coach. Last but not least, is to learn these invaluable skills from a book or a journal.

There are umpteen journals available that are dedicated to the cause of leadership learning. These journals are the only places where one can learn newer and newer ideas. The sole aim of these journals is to work towards better leadership. A number of exponents in leadership training write in these journals.

This valuable advice is otherwise unavailable to everyone. One can exploit the information which is at your fingertip.

With the advent of internet and World Wide Web one can easily access all this information easily. All required information is just one click away. One cannot always have the assistance of a peer or a coach owing to one reason or the other. In such circumstances peer journals are the best way to acquire the information from the journals.

The leadership journals provide you the cutting edge information about the development of leadership. These help you gain a good understanding about what is leadership, the roles of mentors in leadership.

Leadership journals give information about what are the new trends in leadership and the information about communities that can help you to become a good leader.

The journals publish information in various categories like research, practice, commentary, and reviews. You can choose the information as per your needs from these categories.

The research section basically deals with theory based papers that debate and explores the methodological and theoretical issues concerning various issues and disciplines of leadership.

In these sections, you can find commissioned articles by leading authors on various topics related to leadership. They also contain debates about various issues regarding leadership.

The practice section contains some articles form practitioner researchers and academics. The section mainly deals with the practice of leadership among various sectors. These articles are subject to peer review and editorial review. This section is a treasure trove for aspiring leaders.

The commentary section has a provocative, timely and profound commentary on the contemporary leadership issues. This section can help you to keep pace with the changing trends in the area of leadership.

The review section encompasses the valuable information about the book that are of great help for a leader. The reviews are rigorous and concerned with the leadership education.

The articles which have undergone a meticulous peer review certainly help you to decide what you should read in order to keep in touch with modern developments in field of leadership.

Again, it is important to note that though the journals are best mentors' good leadership skills can only be achieved through practice. The journals only take care of the 'intellectual' side of your leadership but the 'action' comes through practice only.

Leadership Seminars

Since leadership can be learned it is better to explore all the ways to learn it. Besides peer guidance, journals, discussions, seminars are a good source to learn the things about leadership.

To go beyond better leadership, you have to inspire your team to achieve the goals. The effective communication is a key to unify a diverse team. You can use the diversity of the group to better advantage. This needs better communication and various seminars held on how to develop your communication skills can help you a lot.

These seminars can help you gain an insight into the dissimilarities between the personalities of the group. You will learn to speak in their language which will create a sense comfort. The seminars help you to assess your style of leadership and to learn adaptation of another leadership styles.

These are helpful to identify and appreciate the varied strengths and challenges. In such seminars, you can learn better strategies to motivate your teammates. This is also useful to locate the essential conditions required for the better productivity.

As Henry Ford has put it, "Coming together is a beginning, keeping together is progress, and working together is success." This needs strong binding of group. This can be achieved by seminars on the goal to be achieved.

The common causes of lack of team spirit are misinterpretation and misunderstandings. To achieve the result, you have to keep the group unified and conducting seminars on various relevant topics is one way to achieve this goal.

In such seminars, you learn to appreciate the challenges the diverse nature of teammates present. The seminars help you learn clarify the diverse expectations and needs that are useful to groom the leadership.

The best advantage of these seminars is that they teach you to minimize conflicts between the teammates of groups. It sheds light on the effective elements of your team.

To be understood and to understand is the single most important factor while leading a team. This needs a focused attempt to learn better communication skills. For such skills, you need to step into the skin of the person you are dealing with.

A good seminar on how people think in and react to certain situations is very useful. It is common misconception of a leader that everybody thinks the way he does. This leads to confusion because people tend to think in their own style and their reactions are quite different from that of yours.

A seminar on interactions with a group can be of great use to understand the thoughts of the group. The aim of a leader is to lead and not to carry away the group. This kind of seminars can give you understanding about not to be carried away by an impulse, even it may seem appropriate at first.

All such seminars will certainly teach you a thing or two about public speaking. Speaking in public is one of the most important assets of a leader. The seminars give you a chance to rehearse your skills before you launch yourself in the field of leadership. Seminars can the best podium to test your oratory skills.

APPENDIX 3: FAMOUS LEADERS

The world has seen a great many leaders in the past. Many great leaders ruled the world. The best ideas are presented by many great leaders in the history.

All the changes that are worth noting are the efforts of many great leaders. Sir Winston Churchill, Martin Luther King Jr., Abraham Lincoln, Mahatma Gandhi, and Margaret Thatcher are some leaders that world has seen.

Sir Winston Churchill was a great historian and statesman. The great leadership skills that he exhibited during wars, has secured him prime place in the British history. He is the best example of how you can overcome shortcomings and acquire a unique place in everyone's heart.

As seen earlier being a good orator is major skill that is needed by a good leader. But Churchill's little stammering has not affected his speeches which has gained him recognition in world history. He was a great politician and eminent personality. He has played an important role during the World War II and the resulting post war coalition. He will be remembered for ages for his role as war time prime minister of Britain.

Martin Luther King, Jr. of USA is another best leader the world has seen. He was a strong supporter of civil rights. He led the first Negro nonviolent demonstration. The bus boycott lasted for 382 days but finally the Supreme Court of United States declared the segregation of Negroes on buses as unconstitutional.

During this campaign, this great leader was arrested and was abused. His house was bombed but in spite of all these hardships he emerged a leader of supreme quality. He was of age thirty when he received the Nobel Peace Prize and he used the sum won to further the movement of civil rights.

Abraham Lincoln is remembered for his leadership in preservation of Union during the Civil War. He is mainly remembered for the beginning of the struggle to demolish the atrocious slavery in United States.

He had characteristic leadership qualities like good oratory skills, great determination and a solid character. He led a simple life. He made great efforts to learn what is needed for good leadership. He struggled to achieve the skills and knowledge while he worked on splitting rails, on farm, and keeping a store.

Mahatma Gandhi was a simple man, who made extraordinary efforts to support India's freedom struggle. Mahatma Gandhi helped India to get freedom from British rule. He achieved this goal with his ingenious leadership style known popularly now as non-violent resistance.

He had charisma and character that him the title Mahatma the great soul. He is also known as the father of Indian Nation. He learned and demonstrated good leadership qualities when he was in South Africa for 21 years.

He led a great movement to secure rights for Indian people in South Africa. He used the tactics of civil disobedience to achieve the goals with success.

Margaret Thatcher has also shown very good leadership qualities. She was prime minister of UK. She was the first woman who ever became prime minister of UK. She was also the longest serving PM in UK. As a leader, know as "The Iron Lady" her decisiveness in the Falklands War turned her into a respected stateswoman on the international stage.

ABOUT THE AUTHOR

Audra Taylor, CPA, has earned the reputation as an innovative leader in the finance space. Currently, she is a dedicated Chief Financial Officer (CFO) and Self-Help & Success Coach who writes and resides in the heart of Phoenix, Arizona.

Hailing from Escanaba, Michigan, her passion for numbers began in grade school. Ultimately, her avid interest in accounting and finance blossomed into mentoring people. However, her love of spreadsheets has remained.

To date, Audra has managed and mentored dozens of talented finance and business professionals, helping them harness their talents so they can pave the path to lasting success. She holds a Bachelor of Science degree in Accountancy from Ferris State University.

Outside of the finance and writing world, Audra loves succulent gardening. In addition, she is an animal welfare advocate. Above all, she enjoys nothing more than spending quality time with her three rescued furry friends, two Rottweilers and one very small, very brave cat.

Keep tabs on Audra; her blog is updated frequently at:
http://www.taylorsuccessjournal.com

See other publications by the author at: amazon.com/author/audrataylor

by Audra Taylor

https://www.amazon.com/Success-Journal-Guided-Journaling-career/dp/1546389652

Journaling helps us figure out who we are, what we want, and can help with decision making and better planning.

The Success Journal is a guided, blank journal to help you find the road to the next stage of your career. The Success Journal also contains sample goals to get you started on your personal journey to better circumvent challenges in your professional or personal life and can help in providing you a stronger sense of fulfillment, joy, and success.

Pages are divided into sections to record goals and steps needed to achieve them, dates to accomplish them by and notes along with inspirational quotes and motivational advice for every chapter.

The Success Journal also contains sample goals to get you started on your personal journey to better circumvent challenges in your professional or personal life and can help in providing you a stronger sense of fulfilment, joy, and success. Journal two days a week for 90 days and help yourself become a more motivated, engaged and focused person with The Success Journal.

Discover your potential with The Success Journal

https://www.amazon.com/Success-Journal-Guided-Journaling-career/dp/1546389652

www.ingramcontent.com/pod-product-compliance
Lightning Source LLC
Chambersburg PA
CBHW071725170526
45165CB00005B/2152